Alfie's Gift

Written by Nette Hilton
Illustrated by Craig Smith

Alfie was tired of living in the drain
down by the beach. The only thing he
liked about it was the smell; he loved to
roll in the sticky, smelly mud and then walk
along the beach with everybody looking
at him.

But the drain was cold in winter and
hot in summer, and Alfie wanted to be
warm and comfortable all year round.

That was what made him decide that it
was time to find a new home: a comfortable
home with chairs to sleep on and slippers
to chew.

Alfie didn't want a home with children in it, though, not after the last time. Christabel Adams had painted him purple once. It had taken four baths before he'd faded to a pale shade of mauve!

And the baby! Alfie shuddered. He could still remember mashed banana oozing down over his ears.

But somewhere, Alfie knew, there was a home for him. And today was exactly the right kind of day for finding it. All he had to do was find a present; it would be polite to take his new owner a gift.

Alfie crossed the beach and scrambled up
to the old dump. There was a rotten old fish
up there that he'd been saving for a special
occasion.

Yes, an old fish would be perfect.

6

As Alfie trotted off he held his head up
proudly and pricked up his one good ear.
(The other one liked to hang down.)

It had been a long time since so many
people had noticed him. Some of them
pointed at him, and one lady even threw
something. But Alfie was too busy to play
fetch. He was on his way to his new home.

It took a while, but eventually Alfie saw
the house that he knew was his.

There was lots of green, green grass, and
there was a porch littered with big chairs, with
plump white cushions swelling out of them.
But best of all, best of all, was the lady.

Alfie almost dropped his fish when he saw
her — just one lady, sitting in the chair
by the little table. She had a cup of tea and
a slice of cake with her, and her eyes were
closed.

Alfie bet — he just bet — that the lady
lived alone. He knew such things. Clever
dogs like Alfie could smell *alone*. He put
his nose in the air and sniffed. It smelled
exactly right.

Alfie was so excited that he pushed
straight through some prickly rose bushes
and headed for the porch — the cushiony
chairs were calling him.

Alfie was polite, though. He didn't disturb
his new owner, even though he was tempted
by her furry sheepskin slippers. Sheepskin
was really nice to chew. Alfie slobbered a
little when he thought about it.

And the cushion. Oh, it was heaven!
Alfie scrunched around and around before
snuggling down with his fish between
his paws.

Alfie was impatient to deliver his present.
But the lady still didn't wake up, so Alfie
dropped the fish on her feet.

His new owner certainly could leap
very high. She danced around, too, waving
her arms. Alfie was pleased. She must have
liked the fish very much.

Then she kicked it. *"Aaaaaagh!"* she said.
Alfie knew that sound. It was the one
people made when they played soccer at
the beach, and *he* knew how to play soccer.

He sprang off the chair and raced after
the fish. It had rolled into a goldfish pond.
The pond was slippery and slimy on the
bottom, but Alfie didn't mind.

He whooshed straight in and then rushed
back onto the porch. He rolled the fish right
up to the lady's chair.

"Goal!" she was supposed to say. But the
lady wasn't there. Alfie waited. Maybe, he
decided, she wanted to play a different
game. She must be hiding so that he could
try to find her.

Alfie ran around to the back of the house.
She wasn't there. He ran back to the front.
She was definitely close by. Yes, there she
was, just inside the door.

Alfie scratched. A little bit of paint
came off, but the door didn't open. Alfie
scratched harder. A bigger bit of paint
came off. She still didn't come out.

Perhaps, Alfie thought, he should leave her alone for a little while. She probably had some important things to do — like shopping for dog food.

Alfie sat down and thought a bit more. He really should do some shopping, too. He slopped his nose into the lady's cup. She had milk in there. Alfie wagged his tail.

He knew exactly where to get milk.

As fast as he could, he raced to the
supermarket. There was always milk there.
He'd seen people carrying cartons of it to
their cars. Alfie didn't like cars, but he wasn't
going to let that stop him from getting the
milk.

He crept along on his belly like a long
crocodile. "Look at that dog!" people said,
and Alfie crept even lower.

His stomach was quite sore by the time he
saw the bag on the back seat of a car.
He scrunched all his muscles until they were
very, very tight — then . . . got it!

Some of the milk spurted out. Some more
slurped out as he ran off. But there was still
some left when Alfie reached his new home;
he could hear it sloshing around in the carton
when he crept back past the rose bushes.

Then Alfie noticed something strange — his cushion was gone! The hard cane chair was empty. But when Alfie noticed that the lady had taken the fish, too, he was pleased all over again. She probably just wanted to play with it by herself.

Alfie gripped his carton tightly as he thought about his new owner in her fluffy slippers, happily tossing the fish in the air.

Alfie barked, just once. He didn't want the milk to stand around for too long and get hot. He heard the sheepskin slippers pad up the hall. Maybe he should put some milk in her cup for her. That would be a good surprise.

It was hard getting up on the table, and even harder getting the milk into the cup. But Alfie managed somehow.

"Good grief!" The lady was so surprised
that she threw her hands in the air and
danced a little dance on her sheepskin feet.
Alfie was delighted.

Then she slammed the door. Alfie was
puzzled. How on earth was he ever going
to sleep on her bed and eat his dog food
if she didn't let him in?

He sat for a long time, right outside the
door. That way he could surprise her when
she came out for their next game.

The moon came up, and still Alfie sat. If
she came out now for a game it would be
too late. And he had nothing to give her
to play with, anyway. She'd probably be sad,
too, if he didn't have another present for her.

Alfie grew sadder and sadder. He didn't even look up when the light went on and the door opened.

"Well, what have you done this time?" The lady had on a fluffy dressing-gown. It was the kind that would flop out when she sat down, so that he could curl up on the bottom bit.

Alfie sighed. She was so kind, and yet he had nothing, nothing at all, to give her. He felt so bad that he didn't even take his head off his paws. He just let his eyes look up at her.

"What a sad sight you are!"
The lady looked at him.
Her mouth wasn't smiling.
Alfie pushed his head lower
on his paws.

If only he had something to give her —
then she might smile. Tomorrow he could
find another fish, but now, right now, all he
had was him.

He looked up at her again. It was no good. She'd never love him now. She'd never give him a home. Alfie smiled a sorry smile.

"Good grief!" The lady bent closer. "Do that again!"

Alfie smiled again. Once he'd seen a smiling dog on a dog food commercial in a television shop window, and he'd taught himself how to smile, too.

The lady stepped onto the porch.

"A smiling dog! What next?" She poked at
him gently with the toe of her slipper.
Alfie smiled harder.

"Well!" she said. "Well, I never!" She shook her head. "I didn't like your fish or your milk, or the mess you made on my cushion. But . . ." She bent down and looked at his face again. "I really like your smile!"

She walked back into the house. "Come
on, dog! I'll get you some dinner!"
And Alfie smiled — a real, happy smile.
He didn't even stop smiling when she gave
him a bath.

He knew that he could always go and roll in
the sticky, smelly mud of his old drain.
Maybe he'd do that tomorrow, or the next
day, or even next week.

But right now it was so much better just
staying here, curled up on the bed, with
his tummy full.